PLANI
A SMALL GARDEN

ROBIN WILLIAMS

HarperCollins*Publishers*

Products mentioned in this book

'Weedol'   contains   diquat/paraquat

Products marked thus *'Weedol'* are trade marks of
Imperial Chemical Industries plc
Read the label before you buy: use pesticides safely.

Editors Maggie Daykin, Susanne Mitchell
Designer Chris Walker
Picture research Moira McIlroy

First published 1988 by
HarperCollins Publishers

This edition published 1992

A CIP catalogue record for this book is available from the British Library.

Photoset by Bookworm Typesetting
Printed and bound in Hong Kong by Dai Nippon Printing Company

Front cover: Clematis montana by Michael Warren
Back cover: Cottage garden by The Harry Smith Horticultural
Photographic Collection

CONTENTS

All gardens are a personal creation. Each will present different problems and require different planning and planting solutions depending on the needs of the owner. Many themes can be adopted, from the incorporation of materials with a Japanese flavour, as shown here, to the use of one or two colours only or allowing a pool or pergola to become the dominant feature.

Given the same plot, ten people would probably arrive at ten distinctly different solutions on how to transform it into their ideal garden. However, what makes a garden a 'good' design is a very personal matter, only the solution which takes into account each person's individual needs and conforms with his or her ideas of beauty may be judged as being well designed.

Some gardens look as if they have evolved entirely on their own without any intervention on the part of the owner but, more often than not, this is the result of very careful planning. 'Natural' gardens of this type are usually built around a very strong, but deliberately disguised framework. Without this framework chaos would result in the form of dense weeds and uncontrollable growth of grass, trees and shrubs and the garden would then cease to exist. On the other side of the coin, some gardens suffer from being over-designed and are unnecessarily fussy, or look contrived. In other words, a 'drawing-board' design consisting, perhaps, of geometric shapes having little relationship to the nature of the plot or the real needs of the owner.

A plan, therefore, is essential; working without one is rather like attempting to paint a picture without a clear idea of the subject matter, and not knowing which medium or colours to use. Unplanned gardens usually turn out to be disappointing and disjointed affairs, though it must be said that some happy accidents do occur when unplanned features and plantings turn out very well but, nevertheless, they are accidents.

Provided the job is tackled sensibly, designing the garden can be enormous fun and very rewarding; even more so when the completed garden has brought the plan to life. The first essential step in the creation of a plan is to make a list of what is required in the garden. It is this that sets the design wheels in motion. List everything – likes or dislikes, the use to which the garden will be put, for example a children's play area, a nature reserve, a place to sun-bathe or a home for plant collections. Don't leave anything out – it's your garden and you want to get the most from it, using the space available to the best effect.

Try to estimate, too, how much time you will have to look after it. If your need is simply for a place to relax, then clearly the amount of maintenance needed to keep the garden in good order must be kept to an absolute minimum. You certainly won't want to be a garden slave, although the maintenance-free garden has yet to be invented! But, nevertheless, certain labour-saving elements can be included in the design. On the other hand, your idea of relaxation may be weeding or cutting grass – a surprising number of people find both these activities therapeutic and relaxing – so, again, this will help to determine the style of garden. Once you have made your list, an overall picture will start to emerge and this may crystallize previous uncertain thoughts as to the

What do you want? Check list

☐ Lawn

☐ Paving

☐ Patio

☐ Rock garden

☐ Pond

☐ Children's play area

☐ Entertaining area

☐ Pets

☐ Screening

☐ Sitting area

☐ Labour-saving

☐ Plant collections

☐ Greenhouse/Conservatory

☐ Vegetables

☐ Fruit

☐ Utility area

garden's shape and form. Decide, too, how much money you have available to spend on the project and over what period of time you intend the development to take place; one will certainly have a bearing on the other. It may be necessary to design the garden into logical or affordable sections or areas to be tackled when time and money permit. Some projects can take as much as four or five years to complete. The important thing is that it is a planned project. Every time you put a spade into the ground or lay a paving slab it will be towards the realization of the plan. This will avoid wasted time and money. Each and every element will go straight to its proper place within the overall scheme.

MEASURING THE GARDEN

Provided the garden is reasonably simple in shape, for example rectangular or square, the measuring should be easy. If the plot is a more complicated shape, then measuring will need more skill, but with the right equipment this is not too difficult. Measuring or surveying presents an obstacle to many people since it has an aura of mystique about it but don't be put off, it is not that difficult.

Before beginning, however, make sure a Site Plan doesn't already exist. For example the plan of the property in the Deeds, obtainable from the solicitor, could be photo-copied, even enlarged to a given scale. An architect's plan may exist, if work has been done on the house which required planning permission. But a word of warning, even if you do have such a plan, take at least one physical measurement to check the accuracy of it. Some of the older Deed plans may not be right.

To be faced with a neglected or almost completely empty garden can be a daunting prospect. Yet given time this site could be turned into a garden similar to the one shown on pages 30–1. It is important to treat the site as a painter would a canvas and to work to a plan based on the design you have created to meet your requirements.

Equipment Assuming no plan exists, it will be necessary to assemble some basic equipment before starting. A tape measure is an obvious requirement, calibrated in metres (metric) or feet (imperial). Some tape measures have both, one at each side of the tape. For medium to larger gardens a 30m/100ft tape is best. For the small garden, a 3m/10ft tape will do. The larger tape can be hired if you feel it will only be required for a single occasion; however, for the subsequent marking out and construction – if you intend to do the work yourself – a tape of your own is fairly essential and will be an investment.

A number of canes or poles to act as markers are useful and some large sheets of graph paper chosen to be compatible with the tape measure – for example, ruled in centimetres/millimetres for metric work and tenths or eighths of an inch for imperial work. An HB pencil and a rubber will be needed. A metric or imperial scale rule is also fairly essential and also a directional compass. For the more difficult shaped gardens a large pair of compasses will be required to fix the corners on the plan. A hard surface on which to place the graph paper will also be useful – a garden table makes the ideal centre for operations.

Making a start Measuring and plotting the results to scale at the time of taking them is better than covering a piece of paper with masses of measurements which have to be disentangled and plotted later. This can lead to measurements being missed out.

The first thing to do when measuring the garden is to pace it out. This gives an approximate idea of size and will help you establish a suitable scale. Choose a scale that will

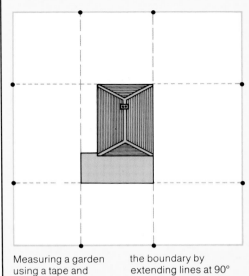

Measuring a garden using a tape and marker canes. The dotted lines are the sighting lines from the house walls to the boundary. You should be able to establish the boundary by extending lines at 90° from the house and measuring them. The boundary is estimated by adding the distance between the marker canes.

allow you to get the whole layout on one sheet of graph paper. For example, 1:100 (10mm to 1m or ⅛in to 1ft) for a medium size garden and 1:50 (20mm to 1m or ¼in to 1ft) for a small garden.

Once you have decided on the scale, start by measuring and scaling down the outline of the house. Don't forget to include windows, door openings, inspection covers, etc. In most houses, walls are straight and corners at right-angles; it is a more difficult proposition if they are not. Having drawn in the house, use the house lines as a base from which to measure the boundaries and corners of the garden. In simply shaped gardens this may be done by 'sighting off' the walls and corners and fixing canes as markers, then measuring off in various directions.

Triangulation With more complicated shapes, triangulation is mostly used. This sounds complicated, but it is simply a method of measuring using a series of triangles based on the house wall lines, the apexes of which fix boundary points and corners. With this method, the pair of compasses is used. (See diagram.)

Measuring to scale on site using either method, or maybe a combination of both, means you have a built-in check, since when corners are plotted they should appear in their right place on the paper. Secondary diagonal check measurements can confirm the accuracy of the measurement. This gives the opportunity to go back over measurements and check if the points are not where they should be. The sighting off, or triangulation, can also position other features within the garden, such as trees and existing path lines, and, by the way, when fixing tree positions don't forget to indicate their spread, since this will subsequently affect the plant choice beneath.

Completing the site plan In an inherited garden, features you do not want to retain need not be included in the site plan, but be very careful about unwanted trees. You may not have a choice about whether or not to retain them if the Local Authority has placed a preservation order upon them. Always check this before removing any tree; not to do so could place you on the wrong side of the law.

Besides the tangible features and elements which may exist in the garden, consider too the less tangible elements, for example, areas of

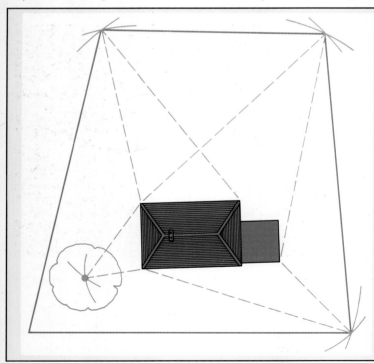

Triangulation is a method used to plot the position of various elements in the garden as well as awkward-shaped boundaries. To establish the position of any point, measure the distance from it to two separate points on the house. Then, using a pair of compasses, draw arcs from the two points with radii corresponding to the two measured distances reduced to scale. Measure the spread of any tree.

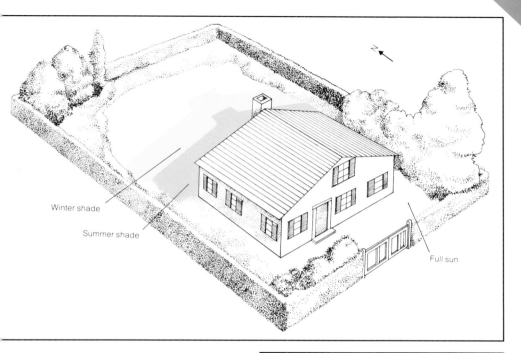

Winter shade

Summer shade

Full sun

shade, areas which are sometimes flooded or remain damp, dry areas, frost pockets, the direction of the prevailing winds. Also consider how features outside the garden could affect your design, for example, overhanging trees, high neighbouring walls, good or bad views.

Orientation This, too, is extremely important, as it dictates the siting of a sitting area, a pond, a shady border, etc. This is where the compass comes into use and the points of the compass should always be clearly marked on the survey and any subsequent plans. You should bear in mind that during the winter the sun is at a lower angle and casts longer shadows. (See above.)

pH One more item of information often overlooked is the soil condition and its pH (the pH being the degree of alkalinity or acidity of the soil).

TOP When drawing your garden plan you should include the orientation so that you know which is the north, and mark in all the areas of sun and shade.

ABOVE This border of bright summer-flowering perennials needs a sunny position. It is ideal for the front of a west-south- or east-facing wall.

9

Soil-testing kits are easy to use and give a good indication of the pH of the soil. The techniques vary slightly with the kit, but most use an indicator fluid which is added to a soil solution and the resulting colour compared against a chart. The pH is read from the colour guide. A low pH (0–6.5) is acid, high pH (7–10) is alkaline and a pH of 6.5–7 is neutral.

Both will have a bearing on the choice of plant material in conjunction with the garden's aspect. Fortunately, easily used and inexpensive testing kits will provide this information. Alternatively, send a small sample of soil to your local horticultural officer, who for a small fee will provide you with a detailed report on its condition and structure. On the other hand, a visual check may be all that is necessary. Plants in adjacent gardens or surrounding countryside will, to some extent, indicate the local pH; for example, rhododendrons, azaleas, pines, birch and brooms will suggest acid soils, whereas the yew, dogwoods, viburnums, field maple, etc, indicate limy conditions. This, of course, is only a rule of thumb. Whether the soil is clay, sandy or loamy can again often be determined visually or when you start to cultivate it.

Levels Finding and establishing levels can present a bit of a problem. However, in smaller gardens there are ways of approximately establishing differences in level. Two are as follows:

• A spirit level laid on top of a straight, measured piece of wood will, when accurately brought to level, provide an indication of a rise or fall simply by measuring the gap between the end which is off the ground and the ground itself. This procedure may be repeated over the entire length of the garden and, when added together, will give the overall fall.

• Panelled fencing may also be used to check levels, provided the panels are the type that are fixed to posts and step down or step up as the ground rises. A simple measurement of the 'steps' either at the top or the bottom, when added together will give the overall and approximate rise or fall. (See diagrams below.)

If the proposed garden is to consist mainly of trees, shrubs and grass, then it is unlikely that level finding will be necessary and the existing ground levels can be left as they are. On the other hand, if the ground slopes and you wish to include areas of level paving and a level lawn, this will inevitably mean the inclusion of steps, slopes and, quite possibly, retaining walls. In this case some idea, at least of the differences in level, is essential in order to calculate the heights of walls for terracing and the number of steps which may need to be included on the plan.

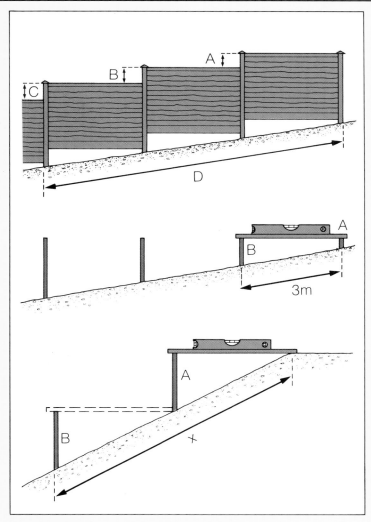

Three methods of establishing levels on a sloping site.

TOP LEFT Measuring the difference in height between either the top or bottom of the fence panels (A, B and C) and adding these together will give the approximate fall over the area D, assuming that the panel tops are level.

CENTRE LEFT Use a spirit level on a straight edge placed on pegs which are hammered into the ground until the tops are level. The difference in height between B and A is the fall in level measured over a distance of 3m/10ft. Repeat this procedure to establish the gradient down the whole slope.

BOTTOM LEFT Using the same method on a steeper slope – A plus B will give the fall in ground over X.

DESIGN PRINCIPLES

There are certain basic principles common to all good design whether it is applied to gardening, architecture or anything else. These principles must each be considered in relation to the others.

The five basic principles are:

- Simplicity
- Unity and harmony
- Balance
- Scale and proportion
- Interest

Simplicity is a very important ingredient, especially where space is limited. It is true that elements of surprise should, where possible, be incorporated, but not if they make a garden over fussy. Simplicity should run through the whole scheme, from the overall plan to the choice of hard materials and plants. Complicated schemes do not induce a sense of calm. Additionally, they will make a small garden look smaller.

Unity and harmony are sometimes difficult to achieve in garden design. Harmony is somewhat subjective, a bit like beauty, depending much upon the eye of the beholder. Nevertheless, unity and harmony in a general sense can be achieved between one element and another, or one group of plants and another within the garden itself and, just as important, between the garden and its immediate surroundings or adjacent architecture. If a garden can, for example, suggest an extension of a house or vice versa, or appear as though both house and garden were designed together, then the result will be far more successful. Unity and harmony between adjacent architecture and the garden may be achieved by selecting materials which are common to both. The

Harmony is demonstrated in this terrace garden where the use of old bricks suits the style of the house and planting.

same or similar bricks or stone of which the house is built could be used in the garden construction in paths or walls. Certain plants with a distinctive form, colour or texture can be repeated in different places. These will bring unity and will help the garden to hang together. How much more restful are planting schemes where colours harmonize, rather than contrast. Some contrasts are good, but not when they become a series of visual shocks.

Balance Many gardens are in a state of imbalance, both from the point of view of structure and colour. Any artist painting a picture will start on the basis of getting the right balance in both these respects. Consider this: in garden planning, what are we doing but painting a three-

Colour balance is an important element in garden design. The garden illustrated has been planted with vibrant, harmonizing colours which create a bright sunny atmosphere whatever the weather.

dimensional picture? Try to avoid placing heavy emphasis on form or colour on one side of the garden only, or at one end or the other. Gardens which slope across the main view are particularly difficult to deal with when it comes to keeping a good balance. Features on the high side will always dominate those on the low side. If levelling is not practical, then the features on the lower side need to be larger or taller or have more impact to achieve a better balance.

Colour balance, too, is important. Bear in mind that bright or vibrant colours should be avoided at the distant end of the view point. These will tend to make a garden look smaller and will be out of balance with, perhaps, less vibrant, pastel colours used in the middle distance or near the house. Generally the best balance is achieved by allowing the colours to cool off as they recede until ultimately we are left with soft whites, blues, greys and dark green at the far end of the garden.

Scale and proportion The horizontal and vertical elements of a garden must be in proportion to its overall size. Often huge weeping willows can be seen growing in quite small gardens, where they dominate everything, including the house. This is an obvious example of bad proportion. In planning the garden, not only must the proportion of flat or horizontal features be considered, but also that of the vertical ones. Paving areas and the units which go into them need to be in proportion: not so small as to make the general area look fussy and not so large as to look ridiculous. Path or patio widths should be in proportion with the size or height of the building with which they are associated (as space will allow). A broad patio behind a tall house will look purposeful and in scale, whereas a narrow patio or path will appear mean and out of scale. Grassed areas look best if they are in proportion with the general area, but are not so large as to make surrounding beds look mean and

Circular lawns create a restful atmosphere in the garden. However, it is difficult to maintain the edge accurately; this problem can be solved with a 'mowing-edge' of bricks set around the lawn and slightly below the level of the grass. This means that the brick edging can be overmown without damage to the mower.

narrow and possibly emphasizing the nearness of the boundary walls or fence.

Squares, broad rectangles, circles and ovals are the best proportions or shapes for creating a sense of calm. Within these shapes, whether paved, gravelled or grassed, there is little or no incentive to move; they

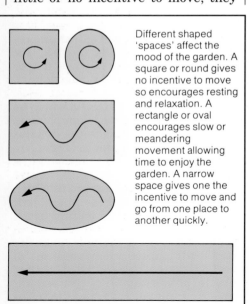

Different shaped 'spaces' affect the mood of the garden. A square or round gives no incentive to move so encourages resting and relaxation. A rectangle or oval encourages slow or meandering movement allowing time to enjoy the garden. A narrow space gives one the incentive to move and go from one place to another quickly.

are just right, in fact, for relaxation. There will, of course, need to be vertical elements surrounding and creating these shapes and the height of these vertical elements (shrubs, hedges, walls, or whatever) will need to be in scale. On the one hand, too low a surround simply makes a ground pattern, whereas too tall a surround confines and oppresses.

Areas which are narrow or long invoke a sense of movement and this sense is heightened when the proportion of the adjacent vertical elements gets higher, until ultimately a passage, or tunnel effect, is achieved. This is good for going places, but does not encourage sitting and relaxing.

Plants, too, need to be in balance and in proportion with each other. Taller plants should not be positioned in front of smaller ones so that the one obscures the other. Tree sizes should be in proportion to the site or adjacent buildings and to each other, so that they do not grow into each other, creating too much shade and claustrophobic conditions.

Interest A garden which combines all the previous four elements but

To create a 'space' as shown on the previous page, the surround must be higher than the eye.

The surround can be of plants or some kind of constructional material. It can be claustrophobic.

Without a high surround, the shape is not a space, it is merely a ground pattern and part of a

bigger area. The 'atmosphere' of the sketch above left does not exist here, and the area looks larger.

Surprise is the secret of interesting garden design. In a small garden this is often difficult to achieve but you should try to include some feature as a talking point. Try

also to prevent the whole garden being seen at one time. Here a beautifully planted terracotta pot provides both a surprise element and a talking point.

lacks interest will be unsuccessful. Some gardens incorporate themes or comprise a series of linking gardens, each with a different character or theme, so that the visitor is led from one area to another. This creates great interest and a sense of exploration. These ideas can, of course, only be carried out in larger gardens, but even the smallest garden can be made interesting. Make sure there is a point of focus – a talking point – perhaps in the form of a sculpture, a pool, a collection of unusual architectural plants. Avoid the possibility of seeing everything at once. Even in the smallest garden try to keep something in reserve, something mysterious, something to be visited. This is not the easiest thing to do in a small space but the careful planting of evergreen shrubs with strong foliage forms will help to provide hidden corners.

DRAWING THE PLAN

After completing the survey or site plan, the most important and possibly the most exciting part of garden design begins. The first step is to check the list made earlier to remind yourself of the features to be included in your ideal garden. The next step is to put a piece of tracing paper over the survey drawing (to protect it as you may make several attempts before you reach the right solution).

Once you have measured and surveyed the garden and decided on the features to include, you can make the plan. This garden has been laid out with a flight of steps as a focal point at the far end, a large area of grass and strong border planting.

On the tracing paper, start to plot in the various features. In other words, make a simple 'functional' plan, all the time referring to the survey drawing beneath. Allow features to fall into their natural place if possible; for example, the main sitting area will most probably be preferred in sun, so if the house faces north and maybe there is an adjacent tree or high building cutting out even more light, then the sitting area will need to be moved further away from the house into the garden. A corner may have been earmarked for a child's play area; but perhaps the survey shows it to be a damp and wet area, so here again this would not be suitable for the original purpose but would be marvellous for a bog garden. The herb garden will, for convenience, need to be near the kitchen, and so on. The various features are like a giant jig-saw puzzle and you will need to move them around until you feel everything is in its rightful and most appropriate place. The various areas will then need to be linked together with paths, grass, pergolas, etc.

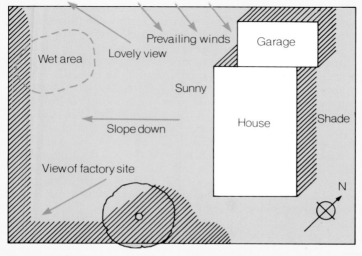

The site analysis or survey drawing is the result of all the observations made when measuring the site. It shows areas of shade, sun, the orientation, information about views and prevailing winds. You should also add in soil pH if relevant and soil type.

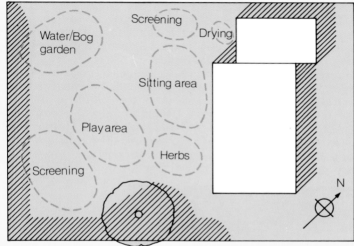

The rough functional plan on which you have plotted in shapes for the garden features you wish to incorporate should look something like this. (Check back to the list on page 5.) The position of features should be related to the site analysis shown above left. For example, it is pointless siting the play area on naturally wet ground or a sitting area in a position of complete shade.

Having decided on the very basic scheme, you can now proceed to specifics. Another piece of tracing paper replaces the functional plan, the latter being kept close to hand for reference. Your outline ideas must now be drawn more accurately to scale to make sure the whole thing works and can be accommodated within the garden area. A good idea is to cut out scale plan models from paper for features such as a shed, greenhouse, sitting areas, a lawn, pool, etc., so that they can be moved around on the tracing paper until you are satisfied with their positions; then you can draw them in. If space permits, paths should accommodate two people walking side by side, and make very good and strong links not only functionally, but visually.

Planting Plan Having established the framework of the garden, which will include all the 'hard' elements, the next stage is the preparation of a planting plan. This will need very careful thought so that good proportion and balance is maintained. In larger schemes, groups of the same plant or shrub are much better than individual plantings, which will only result in spottiness. Get hold of several catalogues with plenty of coloured photographs. Good catalogues will also give ultimate tree, shrub and plant sizes, flowering seasons, berries and fruiting seasons and other descriptions, even planting distances, so you know how many of a particular plant is needed to fill a specific area.

Check the pH of the soil and the soil conditions to make sure the shrub you have chosen will thrive in the particular location in which you wish to place it. Have regard too, to the aspect; for example, whether the shrub or tree will be in shade or sun.

Don't fall into the trap of going into the garden centre or nursery and choosing plants at random. Do your research first and always know exactly what you are going to buy before you go. Plants as gifts are fine, provided they conform to a planting plan, otherwise they may be a problem. Above all, choose plants that will give all-year-round pleasure as much as possible – this is especially important in the small garden. Some gardens look wonderful in the spring but are dull in summer. Consider how a plant will look out of its flowering period – which may be short – it's important. Much of the gardener's pleasure comes from watching the changing of the seasons, so avoid a predominance of evergreens. These will make for a static garden and if overdone are positively funereal. Most evergreens, however, make excellent foils for other deciduous shrubs and some, of course, are extremely beautiful in their own right, rhododendrons and camellias for example.

Try to achieve a good balance between the hard, or constructed, elements and the planting of the garden. Unfortunately, the hard elements are instant and it may be some years before the plants assume their correct proportion, but it is worth waiting for.

The choice of plants is very much a matter of personal preference and colour is one important factor you must consider. Here, lavender and roses are complemented by green and silver foliage to make a delicate and fragrant plant association.

REALIZING THE PLAN

On completion of the plan, naturally you will now be keen to see the garden in reality, but first you must decide whether or not you have the time, inclination, or skill, to do all the work required yourself.

Generally speaking, garden 'Do it Yourselfers' find the cultivation of beds and planting of various trees, shrubs and plants comparatively easy, but baulk at the idea of laying paths, building walls, etc. There is no doubt skill is needed for this, so the really determined could attend a short garden construction course at one of the local colleges, or obtain the help and advice of a builder friend. D.I.Y. is obviously cheaper than engaging the services of a landscape contractor. Construction costs are normally divided into half for materials and half for labour. Most landscape contractors are very amenable and do not mind carrying out part (perhaps the most difficult parts) of the work, with the rest being done by yourself.

Before engaging the services of any landscape contractor, as with any trade, check out credentials and obtain references. Members of B.A.L.I. (British Association of Landscape Industries) are generally very reliable and will normally give a free quotation for the work. As with all work, there will be a logical sequence of events, but it is always a good idea not to rush to clear out an inherited, or established garden. There may be horticultural goodies lurking beneath the soil or beneath overgrowing shrubs or trees, which you would be pleased to keep. Wait a few months to see what grows. Plants can, with care, normally be transplanted to conform to new areas shown in your plan, so use the planning time for observation also. Mark any plants you decide to keep.

Roses again, this time in shades of pink and red, with a more striking contrast provided by the yellow-green flowers of *Alchemilla mollis*.

Alchemilla is a doubly useful plant because when not in flower it has very decorative foliage. It will grow in sun or partial shade. It also self-seeds.

At the appropriate time, the first job after clearing the ground is to measure and mark out the garden in accordance with the plan and this can be done with the help of string, poles or sand, the sand being trickled along the ground to form lines. Usually the hard elements of a garden are the first to go in, together with any associated levelling or earthworks. The hard elements will normally dictate final soil levels. Cultivation (digging the planting areas and adding manures and fertilizers) and lawn laying come next, with planting last. In front gardens, drive surfacing is the last.

Years ago, planting was confined to the late autumn and winter months, but with the production of container-grown plants many small trees, shrubs and herbaceous plants may now be planted at almost any time of the year other than during a very dry spell of weather.

THE SLOPING GARDEN

Sloping sites bring with them particular problems, but when these are overcome, the gardens constructed on such sites are often more interesting than those planted on the flat. The main difficulties encountered when dealing with a sloping site are listed below.

- Getting up (or down) the slope, either on foot or with machinery.
- On severe slopes the absence of flatter areas for sitting or children's play area.
- On certain soils, the drainage may be either too good or very poor.
- Maintenance.
- Soil migration.

Terracing The first inclination when dealing with a sloping site is to terrace it, but this can bring its own problems. In terracing, the areas between the newly created flat surfaces will, in consequence, be steeper than ever, possibly necessitating the building of costly retaining walls or some other retaining structures. There will no doubt be considerable excavation necessary too. Can the excess soil be removed? At what cost?

The second, equally important, consideration in terracing will be the visual effect. From a standing position, normally one's eyes follow a slope up or down and most of the sloping surface can be seen, but once the same slope has been terraced, little can be seen beyond the first or second embankment or wall supporting the flat surfaces. The garden has in effect, been 'terraced' out of

A low, raised bed at the foot of the balustrade is home to a selection of alpines and dwarf conifers. The steps leading down from the terrace are given added interest by being lined with pots of fuchsias. This is an alternative way of coping with a change in level to the one shown in the garden illustrated on pages 22-3.

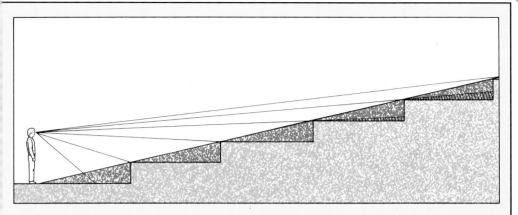

The whole of a surface which slopes in either an upwards or downwards direction can be seen without any difficulty by someone standing below or above it. Once the surface has been terraced, little can be seen beyond the first or second level. The flat areas between terraces have been effectively lost.

sight and much of the impact lost.

Designing a sloping garden needs extra care to create the fine balance between the need to have usable flat surfaces with a good visual effect. Slopes either up or down, however, are easier to cope with than slopes which go across the main view, and which can look as if they are sliding down into the next door garden. A careful balancing act is needed to avoid this with extra 'weight' or 'height' being given to the lower side. This is discussed under 'balance' on page 12.

Plan One

The garden on page 22 slopes not only downwards, but also to some extent across near to the house, which is not an unusual situation. Broad paved areas close to the house permit family use and entertaining, even when the ground beyond may be wet. Steps in conjunction with flat areas overcome the differences in level. Steps in the garden need to be fairly shallow, say, based on multiples of 15cm (6in) high – the risers –

and fairly deep 45cm (18in) – the treads – to provide a comfortable ascent or descent, with a landing for pausing or resting every ten steps or so. Step treads and paved areas should have a non-slip surface. Quite often one sees paving slabs laid, for some mysterious reason, with the smooth side uppermost. This can be very dangerous especially following rain or during icy conditions. The various retaining walls take care of the differences in level and are at a suitable height near the terrace to provide extra seating. Retaining walls need to be equivalent to one third their height in

Mowing-edge

This is formed by a course of bricks laid around the lawn slightly below the level of the grass so that it does not interfere with mowing. The mower can, therefore, be used over the edge of the grass. A mowing-edge is especially useful against a wall or step. See page 14

A focal point needs to be carefully sited. In the garden illustrated above and right, the sundial has been placed on the main axis line. Roses are a good choice for a part of the garden not immediately visible, being very colourful and fragrant in summer while the bare winter stems cannot be seen from the house. It is important to plant some evergreens for winter interest; position some on the level nearest to the house where they will help to screen the rest of the garden.

thickness to be strong, and should have a deep foundation. They also need to be well drained at the rear.

The large circular lawn and adjacent paths create an atmosphere of peace and tranquillity. Geometric shapes like these need to be preserved, as subsequent uneven edging can soon destroy the symmetry. Mowing-edges set just below the level of the grass will help to maintain the shape as well as reducing the need for frequent edge trimming. From this area we are led by carefully positioned steps and a central path through a lower area. This area could have a different theme, it might be planted as a rose or iris

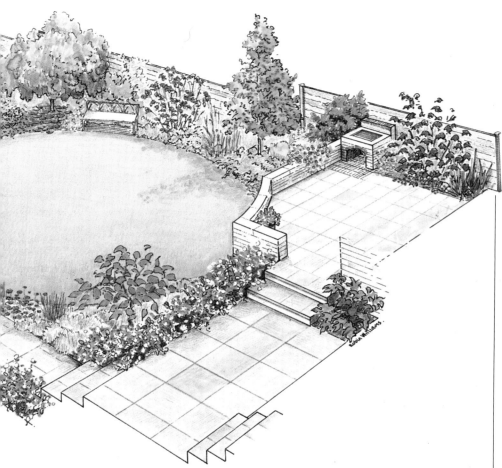

garden for example. It is sufficiently removed from immediate view so that in winter you will not be looking at bare earth or pruned roses. The focal point (bird bath) at the middle centre is a very important feature, as it is sited on the main axis line of the garden. It is the point to which our eyes go, having travelled across the various components of the garden, and at the same time it links those various areas together and has a unifying effect.

Finally, the bottom area provides vegetables or salads and a work area. On maturity, this last section of the garden would be completely obscured from view by various trees and shrubs, or you might prefer to include a hedge – but not privet.

The unadorned fences surrounding the plot actually emphasize the slope, so climbing and wall plants will, in time, obscure them completely and provide a much better back drop to the entire garden.

THE SEASIDE GARDEN

The seaside garden has a distinct character which is born out of coastal weather conditions. Plants and materials need to be tough to withstand winter gales, salt-laden winds (effective up to five miles inland) and even sea spray, depending on the proximity of the garden to the sea. Should the house and garden be used only at weekends or during the summer holidays, then this will have a bearing on the choice of materials which, in turn, will affect the overall design, since a need for low maintenance would be an overriding factor.

Gardens in coastal areas offer the gardener an opportunity to grow some of the less hardy garden plants. Here, a sub-tropical atmosphere is created by the choice of plants – kniphofia (red-hot poker), phormiums and a *Cordyline australis* palm

It will be necessary to choose plants which tolerate drought as well as resisting salt winds. The use of grass as ground cover must also be carefully considered should no one be at hand to carry out watering and mowing during the summer. Fortu-nately, most large nurseries publish in their catalogues a list of trees, plants and shrubs which will tolerate seaside conditions; many of these have silver or grey leaves.

Larger gardens may need to have a 'shelter belt' to reduce the effects of

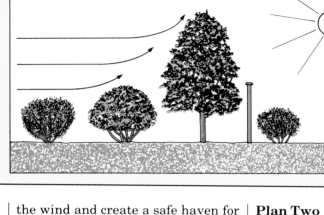

Although seaside gardens are warmer than those inland, they can suffer badly from wind damage. This problem can be solved by establishing a shelter belt of shrubs and trees to deflect and filter the wind before it reaches the garden fence or wall. Shelter belts are also useful for inland gardens.

the wind and create a safe haven for the plants. Shelter trees such as sycamore, thorn, whitebeam, cupressus and pines must be planted when fairly small to succeed under these conditions. Large nursery trees or semi-mature trees are very difficult to establish in exposed situations. High solid fences and walls used on their own without a shelter belt of trees are not usually a good idea for coastal situations since, in high winds, so much turbulence is created on the supposedly sheltered site that severe damage to plants can result from downward blowing air currents. A combination of tree and shrub 'shelter belt' and fence or wall is the best solution, since the force of the wind will be reduced by the trees and shrubs before it arrives at the face of the fence or wall. On the credit side, seaside gardens can, once given protection and shelter, provide a home for many semi-hardy plants which would not grow inland, since frosts are not a regular feature of seaside gardens, the air temperature being moderated by the more even sea temperatures. The soil, however, is probably light, apt to dry out quickly and lacking in nutrients. It will need to be improved by feeding.

Plan Two

The garden illustrated on the next page is more or less square, perhaps fronting a fisherman's cottage; although it might equally well be at the back. Around the plot are strong walls, built of local stone. Materials used in a garden should, if possible, always be chosen to harmonize with the local environment; stone is therefore especially suited to the seaside. A path of old bricks, or setts, leads straight from the gate to the front door, with another path at an angle of 90 degrees to it servicing a seat (the wall has been left out of the drawing in order to allow the seat to be seen).

The central focal point is an old

Bricks

Do not choose bricks which are too smooth, especially on sloping paths; ice or rain will make them dangerous. It is not entirely necessary to lay bricks on mortar, new techniques have been developed where baked clay or concrete bricks are laid on a sharp sand base, with butted joints, where only the edging bricks need to be set in cement.

Gravel, pebbles and boulders are a natural part of the seaside scene and many can be collected from beaches. A combination of pebbles and gravel makes a good labour-saving alternative to grass, especially where, as here, it is interplanted with succulents such as echeveria and mesembryanthemum. The latter can be raised from seed each year. Overwinter echeverias indoors.

White, yellow and mauve are good colours to use in the seaside garden as they reflect the bright light and atmosphere. This spectacular collection of flowering annuals and grasses must be raised from seed each year. Tagetes, pot marigolds, lobelia, ageratum, petunia and iberis are among the plants included.

stone sundial and this is intended to be viewed from four directions, the gate, the front door, the seat and the conservatory or garden-room. In fact, the garden revolves, as it were, round the sundial. Enough space has been left to allow for easy movement around the sundial and the lavender surrounding it acts as a frame and links the sides of the path together. Grass is not used, since this would be difficult to keep in good condition; instead, gravel or small pebbles cover the ground and, in this instance anyway, are far more appropriate than grass. In addition to the pebbles, larger boulders make interesting sculptural forms and are sur-

resident gardener some really beautiful effects can be achieved using bright annuals in window boxes and beds as well as herbaceous plants, but all of these require regular care and watering.

This garden would work equally well away from the seaside. A change in plant selection and materials may have to be made to link with local buildings and architecture, but the principles of the design remain. However, the inclusion of plenty of silver, white, mauve and yellow plants would preserve its seaside character reflecting bright light and sun.

rounded by low, carpeting plants such as saxifrage, thyme and sedum. The taller shrubs which grow against the walls, enjoying the protection they give, include atriplex, hebe, escallonia, olearia and many others; even cordylines and various hardy palms could be planted in sheltered, sunny corners. For the

THE TOWN GARDEN

Town gardens are often quite small and confined, with the smallness being emphasized by obvious boundaries of high walls or fences. These, in turn, create large areas of shade in comparison with the size.

In older gardens the soil may be sour, or worn out by intensive use. Access to the garden can be difficult, especially if there is no rear gate for then everything must be taken through the house. If much clearance work needs to be done the debris will have to be removed through the house too, since many local authorities prohibit garden fires within urban areas. All these points are on the debit side. On the credit side, rear garden 'gems' exist in many towns simply because they were thought out and carefully planned first.

There are two basic ways in which a town garden can be tackled. First by taking the boundary walls or fences and making them part of the plan, in other words adopting a formal approach. The second way is

LEFT An abundance of colourful plants imparts a cottage-garden atmosphere to this well-established town garden. The path entices the visitor to move down the garden to see what other delights are in store. The planting is varied and includes catmint, roses, campanulas, clematis, foxgloves and delphiniums.

RIGHT This bold and effective plant association for an area that gets some sun is composed of *Hosta crispula,* the white, bell-like flowers of *Polygonatum* × *hybridum* and the deep blue, early summer-flowering cornflower, *Centaurea montana.*

to make the garden into a jungle by obscuring the boundaries completely, so that to all intents and purposes there are none. Each approach has pros and cons. The former will make the best of the sunny areas, such as they are, and is more suitable for family use and play, since it permits larger areas of flat paving or lawn. The jungle approach, inevitably, will create even more shade, but will look better, especially from the house, a 'stage set' if you like; but flat useable areas will need to be reduced to accommodate larger planting areas, for to achieve the best effect the planting will need to be quite bold and varied.

Soil With all town gardens, because of restricted access, soils are better improved than changed. Bear in mind that materials like soil and sand bulk up to 30 per cent on digging, so this must be taken into the calculation if a soil change is being considered. A generous dressing of compost and fertilizer and lime can work wonders with old soil. Go easy on the lime though, until the soil pH has been established. This can vary wildly in the smallest town garden from being very limy (high pH) next to old boundary walls (where, over the years, old-fashioned

This shady corner has been given a Japanese feel by the use of several large, rounded boulders softened by a small thicket of evergreen bamboo. The gate is made of bamboo canes lashed together and the wall is painted white. A simple yet effective idea that is easily copied.

deteriorating lime mortar has gone into the soil, or builders' rubble has been buried) to being quite acid (low pH) due to the action of rain bringing down in solution chemicals resulting from pollution.

Screening In the smallest town gardens you will want a place to sit, preferably in the sun, but ideally where you will not be overlooked. Unfortunately, this is sometimes very difficult to achieve, especially if adjacent houses are tall. Any attempt to put a conventional roof over the sitting area will be counterproductive since it will keep out the sun as well as the neighbours' eyes. A pergola with appropriately spaced and orientated crossbars will often overcome this problem since, when

An interesting corner which offers many ideas to the keen gardener. The pool with its single jet fountain is set into a low, circular raised bed planted with a mixture of ground cover, including dwarf conifers and herbs. Stylish garden furniture set under a tiled arbour adds a further touch of contrasting colour.

Shade is often a problem in the small garden but if it is regarded as an asset and planted accordingly it can become a most attractive feature.

Many of the shade-loving plants have large leaves and when massed together they create a luxuriant and tranquil atmosphere that is especially welcome in town.

viewed obliquely from, say, adjacent high windows, it presents a series of overlapping bars to the viewer, whilst those sitting beneath it are able to look up to open sky through the bars, at the same time losing little direct sunlight. Some gardens are so small that a patio is all that can be accommodated. Even this can be made exciting with well placed planters and climbing plants, the latter taking up very little room but softening the hard appearance.

the width. The terrace, or patio, is positioned against the house to gain as much privacy as possible and, in this example, it is a natural sun trap, especially after midday. The pergola screens the area from an overlooking neighbouring house extension. Pebbles or gravels make an interesting and labour-saving ground cover and stepping stones lead from the terrace to the side path and direct the eyes to the focal point statue. In front of the statue is an area of green; this could be grass, or even a low-growing plant such as *Minuartia caespitosa* (in sun) or *Arenaria balearica* (in shade).

Behind the statue is a semi-circular and light-reflecting pool, framed on three sides by water-associated plants, such as bamboo and iris. These need not be water or bog plants in reality, but should look as though they were (since the water in the pool will be contained within the liner). A shed is inconspicuously positioned so that it is almost entirely screened from view. A balanced planting scheme of shrubs and small trees provides all-year-round interest in the side borders with spots of bright colour supplied by annuals growing in pots placed in various positions throughout the garden.

Separating the garden into distinct areas, as has been done here, creates an illusion of greater space. It also adds variety and interest.

Trees for small gardens, especially when used for screening, must be choosen with the utmost care and need to be in proportion with the site, otherwise the problem of unattractive outside features will be replaced by even more shade within and difficult growing conditions beneath tree canopies. A simple rule is that the closer you place the screen to the main point of view, the more effective it will be.

Plan Three

The town garden illustrated is typical of many situated behind semi-detached houses. The garden is quite narrow, and long in comparison to

THE COTTAGE GARDEN

Traditionally, the English cottage garden is a cheerful, colourful and seemingly accidental arrangement of flowers consisting mainly of annuals or herbaceous perennials with occasional shrubs like forsythia or old-fashioned roses and, perhaps, the odd fruit tree.

There appears to be no form, no set pattern. Plants are exchanged, given by friends or neighbours, sometimes taken from the wild, then planted where there is a space. Paths are either gravel or paving flags, again randomly placed, using local, inexpensive materials: all very nostalgic.

Many people would love to have such a garden, but are prevented from doing so because of the need to spend a lot of time keeping it under control. A contradiction perhaps, since in appearance it would seem that very little time has been spent in maintenance. This is certainly not true, as any cottage garden

Growing a wide variety of plants is the delight of having a cottage garden. Here the vivid blue of *Geranium* 'Johnson's Blue' is complemented by violas, white phlox, love-in-a-mist, pink roses and the bright yellow creeping jenny, *Lysimachia nummularia* 'Aurea'. Such a display must be kept in good order to be visually appealing.

owner will confirm. Nevertheless, there is such charm in this type of garden, perhaps it's all worth the effort. Even the apparently unplanned cottage garden, though, needs to be designed, or at least a framework provided within which to work. A garden could well be in essence a cottage garden with labour-saving elements contained inconspicuously within it.

Plan Four
The garden on pages 34-5 has 'tapestry' paving making the terrace – not a patio in an English cottage garden. By 'tapestry' paving I mean various paving materials, such as old stock bricks, setts, paving flags, slate or clay tiles, which have been reclaimed and arranged randomly. Age and weathering will reduce any undesirable colour contrasts and the terrace will then complement the surrounding planting rather than vie with it. Carpeting plants grow in colourful profusion from occasional cracks or holes deliberately left open between the various paving materials. It is a good idea to keep the

plants to the outside areas since tables and chairs will, no doubt, be placed towards the centre of the terrace for outdoor entertaining and enjoying the view.

A path runs along the shady side of the garden, releasing the other, sunny side, for more planting, and eventually reaches the vegetable garden through a clipped evergreen arch. This arch and the hedge could be of yew, which is rather slow growing, or of privet, preferably in its golden form. Certainly a cottage garden associated plant, if there is such a thing, would be more in

This charming vegetable and herb garden can be seen at Barnsley House in Gloucestershire. Lavender and standard roses add colour and interest to a fascinating garden which is a source of ideas for anyone prepared to plant in this detailed manner.

A vegetable plot need not be simply functional. The choice of what to grow should be made with some consideration to appearance as well as productivity. Well grown vegetables, as can be seen here, are as attractive as flowering plants. Nasturtiums and all kinds of herbs will add a touch of colour to the garden as well as livening up the cooking.

keeping than a modern, coniferous type of hedge such as *Cupressus × leylandii.* Alternatively, the arch and hedge could be replaced by a wooden structure covered with climbing plants.

The vegetable garden is functional, a no-nonsense affair and, therefore, needs to be screened, as does the greenhouse. With a little imagination, however, a formal vegetable garden could be designed, perhaps in various simple patterns and edged with box or lavender. This

Delphiniums are many people's idea of the perfect summer flower, especially when they are seen, as here, in a wonderful array of mauves and blues. Pale yellow, white and pink varieties are also obtainable but in some ways these colours do not seem to suit the plant so well. Given a well manured, deeply dug soil and a position in full sun, delphiniums will dominate any plant association.

would then be a place worth visiting for its own beauty.

The height of the hedges, or fences, surrounding the garden will, to some extent, determine the amount of shade within it. Modern fences take a long time to weather or become sufficiently covered in plants to integrate them successfully into the cottage-garden ideal. A very useful fence for instant effect is the wattle or osier type, made from woven hazel or willow branches. This makes a wonderful foil, too, for all kinds of shrubs and plants.

The small pond is home to newts and frogs and is the watering place for birds and bees and other insects. This can be made fairly simply and inexpensively with a flexible liner and is surrounded by randomly placed stones. Several cross paths are functional, yet provide interest, whilst a pergola accommodates a favourite climbing plant, perhaps a honeysuckle, rose, *Clematis montana* or wisteria; it also screens an awkward corner.

THE NATURE GARDEN

In gardening circles, there has, in recent years, been a strong 'back-to-nature' call, with much emphasis on ecological and wild life gardens. This idea is not confined to gardens, and large scale schemes are under way throughout the country; motorway embankments, verges, are obvious examples of this. Once they were manicured regularly, but now are left to grow naturally, so encouraging an abundance of wild life.

There is no reason whatsoever why such ideas may not be incorporated into gardens on a domestic scale. The natural, wild appearance, however, is not achieved by accident, nor can things really be left to nature; to do so would probably result in a thicket, where possibly three or four plant species would become dominant in a very short space of time, to the detriment, and possibly extinction, of all others. These natural or wild gardens need to be just as carefully planned and maintained as the most formal or sophisticated garden. The owner,

It can be difficult to make a nature or plant collector's garden work effectively as a good design. To do so requires a strong basic plan and a reason for grouping plants together. Here a raised gravel bed is home for a collection of alpine and rock plants. An attractive feature in itself, perhaps edging a patio, it also provides ideal growing conditions for this type of plant.

LEFT The unexpected adds interest. An unusual statue tucked away under a tree makes a background for a group of Welsh poppies, *Meconopsis cambrica.*

quite understandably, will wish to have many different species of wild or indigenous plants and, most likely, in combination with the best of the not so wild. In time, these will bring a wider variety of insects, birds and butterflies, if this is the object of the exercise.

Plan Five

Being on a domestic scale, the garden on page 38 needs to accommodate people as well as plants and wild life and a terrace, or sitting area, has been incorporated for this purpose. To be in keeping with the general scheme, the materials have been chosen to integrate well – bricks and weathered natural paving, practical, yet unobtrusive. Ground cover in the main areas is provided by grass or gravel, each accommodating appropriate and associated plants. Incidentally, in larger gardens, areas of grass may be left to grow to encourage different species of meadow plants. This idea becomes a practical one if there are regularly mown paths passing through these areas, while the remainder is left to set seed and also to allow any interplanted bulbs to ripen naturally.

Rockeries and pools can be combined to accommodate plants which need well-drained situations, such as stonecrop and thrift, with bog plants such as wild astilbe, irises, the

A woodland area in a semi-shaded corner. Rhododendrons and foxgloves contrast against the delicate flowers of aquilegia. The last two are self sown.

37

marsh marigold and primulas.

The pond itself should be as natural looking as possible, ideally with about 15cm (6in) of clay spread over the Butyl or concrete lining. On the other hand, if it is possible to excavate a natural pond in retentive clay, then so much the better.

This garden could equally well accommodate the more sophisticated trees and plants of the plant collector rather than those of the naturalist. Many of our so-called natural, or indigenous, trees and shrubs are imports anyway from centuries ago.

Indeed, some cultivated forms have escaped back into the wild and are now considered to be indigenous.

With any plant collection, it is fairly essential to have a strong ground pattern, especially if the plants are placed together with

cultural requirements overriding the need to associate them for their colour or texture. Without careful thought given to the overall basic garden design and the need to link features together, the plants lack unity and balance and the garden is unsuccessful. The ground pattern and use of vertical elements is all-important to this kind of garden. Planting areas should be linked together with paths, areas of grass, steps etc., to form a strong skeleton on which the plants themselves will form the flesh.

A pool is a useful feature in a garden devoted to plants as it can be used to link areas together as well as providing a natural habitat for water and bog plants. As in the main illustration, this one is incorporated in a rock garden and interest is held by well placed trees and the variegated grass.

THE EASY-CARE GARDEN

The easy-care garden is one that will be appreciated by those who like all the benefits of a garden – beauty, scent, tranquillity, a place to entertain or, perhaps, for children to play games – without the attendant maintenance problems. Perhaps time is at a premium and there is little opportunity to attend to the garden. Some people actually dislike 'gardening' but enjoy the benefits that the garden brings.

In both these instances the easy-care garden comes into its own. The design should eliminate fussy lines, and difficult-to-maintain surfaces, plants which need lots of attention and so on, to ensure success. Such gardens must, by definition, include large areas of paving and often raised flower beds, mowing edges and so on. In the main, because of the higher cost of construction in relation to that of plants and planting, gardens which include a high proportion of hard materials are more expensive to create. Built-in irrigation systems are often a feature of this type of garden and although a good reliable system can be expensive, it is a great time saver. The seep hose is a good alternative.

'Hard' landscaping and easily grown, trouble-free plants are important factors in a labour-saving garden, but this does not mean that the garden lacks interest. In the illustration a stone seat has been incorporated in a raised bed planted with rhododendrons, azaleas, grasses and hostas, all plants requiring very little maintenance once they are established.

A combination of different textures of paving, gravel and small boulders with easy-care ground cover plants makes an interesting but easily maintained garden feature. Gravel can be kept weed free by the use of weedkiller such as 'Weedol'.

Plan Six

The hedges in the garden on page 42 need to be very carefully chosen in terms of the plants used, since some plants need to be regularly clipped. A stone or brick wall would be a better idea or even a timber screen. But even with the latter, painting with preservative needs to be carried out every few years. For a garden to be truly labour saving, it would inevitably consist entirely of stone, brick or concrete, so in most instances a compromise is reached and plants are introduced for their softening effects.

The patio and associated path is flat, with an easily brushed surface, and is large enough to accommodate table and chairs with enough space around them for movement. A brick-built barbecue is also featured. The lawn is flat, with an uncomplicated shape, and the paving is set slightly below the level of the grass to eliminate regular edging and to allow the mower to pass over without damage. Mowing edges (hidden beneath foliage) enclose the lawn on

the remaining sides, preserving its shape. These may be of brick or flat stone, again set at a level to permit overmowing. A simple pergola creates interesting patterns of light and shade, whilst hosting favourite climbing plants. The furthest area is

A wooden deck leads on to a gravelled area. Choose a durable, unwarped wood for the deck and treat it with a preservative, although as it is above ground level air can circulate and it is less likely to rot.

a small salad garden which includes a greenhouse; neither is too large, and both are easily managed. In severe 'anti-gardening' cases, these could be left out altogether.

The trees and other planting are all good no-nonsense varieties, but even so, have been carefully planned to give the best effect. Mulching all the beds between the various plants with 'Forest Bark' Chipped Bark, compost, peat or even gravel, will reduce weeding to the absolute minimum and as a bonus will benefit the plants too. Any existing weeds must be eliminated before the application of any such mulches. Use a weedkiller such as 'Weedol' for annual weeds or glyphosate for more persistent kinds. Mulching is a useful way of controlling weeds which looks good as well as being effective.

A grass lawn, especially in a small, shady garden, is not always a good idea, both from a maintenance and a cultivation point of view. Useful alternatives are small-leaved ivies, lesser periwinkle, and other low-growing evergreen plants. They do not always provide such a regular textured surface, but can look very attractive, certainly better than patchy grass. Pea shingle or gravel is another obvious ground cover which contributes to a garden's character and, best of all, doesn't need cutting or feeding.

The easy-care garden should allow time for sitting and entertaining. So why not do this in style and install a barbecue area? This one even has a raised herb bed within easy reach of the cook. The barbecue itself can be constructed from bricks and has a built-in cupboard to hold fuel.

THE WALLED GARDEN

Because of the prevailing high land prices, gardens, especially those within new developments, are becoming smaller. Accordingly, there has been an increased interest in what has come to be known as the patio, or walled, garden. Gardens like this acquire character as they age.

Walled gardens are not new: the very first gardens were walled, giving protection against animals, thieves, and providing a haven for herbs, vegetables and the recreational pursuits of the owners. However, these were generally fairly large in size and today's walled, or patio, gardens are much smaller. As previously mentioned, high walls surrounding small spaces immediately cause problems of shade. On the credit side privacy and a feeling of security are gained. The garden illustrated must be typical of many thousands up and down the country, if not with a wall, then certainly with a high fence, so the general principles will apply.

Plan Seven

The first requirement of this type of garden is to open it up visually and remove any sense of enclosure. The introduction of an uncomplicated, light-reflecting ground surface makes a good start. This can be of light-coloured paving slabs, areas of

A pergola or arbour provides shade, shelter and privacy, as well as being a focal point in the garden. It can be planted with a wide variety of flowering or non-flowering climbers, even, if it's sunny enough, with a grape vine, and then you can also enjoy the fruit.

A walled garden can be given a Mediterranean atmosphere by including a collection of plants in containers. This colourful display is of pelargoniums, petunias and lobelias.

grass (although this may not be a practical proposition for reasons of size and access), areas of light coloured gravel and so on.

An 'L'-shaped pool positioned next to the house, from which it can be readily seen and enjoyed, is a wonderful light reflector and increases the sense of space. The inside of the pool in a formal situation is better painted black. This enhances the mirroring effect of the water's surface; light colours do not, and the bottom and sides can be readily seen. Seats play an important part in a walled or patio garden, either permanently positioned, where they double up as focal points, or as portable units which can follow the sun around. Walls around raised beds also make good extra seating, provided they are approximately 30cm (12in) wide and 45cm (18in) high. Cushions make them more comfortable as seats.

Depending upon the orientation of the garden, which will determine the choice of plants, walls and fences make ideal hosts for a wide variety of shrubs and climbers. Warm sheltered walls may even allow the cultivation of choice tender subjects such as acacia or fremontodendron. Wisterias enjoy the comparative

Paving and pebbles provide the background for an assortment of terracotta pots. This simple combination is very effective and can be used to add interest to an otherwise shady corner. Many plants could be used in such a collection including hostas, grasses, ivies and miniature bamboos. Some, as shown here, can also be encouraged to root between the cobbles, and to allow for this the cobbles have been laid loose.

45

A bright sunshade and tablecloth add a touch of colour to a shady and cool garden. This is an ideal setting for some of the dramatic and luxuriant shade-loving plants such as bamboos and mahonias. Fatsia, hostas and ferns would also be good in this situation. As it is too dark to grow many water plants successfully, the pool has been lined with pebbles which will reflect light from the water's surface.

Wisteria can be spectacular trained over a pergola. Some strains however, do not flower easily and may be disappointing. Other good climbers for this purpose include Clematis montana, the white jasmine, *Jasminum officinale*, a climbing rose such as 'Albertine' or 'Zephirine Drouhin', one of the vines or a large-leaved variegated ivy.

shelter of the walled garden too and can be grown over a large pergola to create an interesting walkway. Even in a small garden like the one illustrated it is important to create views and cross vistas. Here the small stone obelisk on a plinth acts as a focal point when viewed from the seat opposite and is framed by the pergola supporting posts. The whole atmosphere is light and airy, even to the extent that the walls have been painted, or rendered, in a light colour to increase light reflection. The addition of lighting would be an excellent idea, extending the garden's use well into the evening.

Walled gardens are improved tremendously by the introduction of plants in containers. Depending upon the atmosphere being created,

these could be terracotta, timber, or imitation concrete. Usually, pots have a foundation plant planted permanently, normally an evergreen type to carry it right through the year, then seasonally these are supplemented with bedding plants, annuals, bulbs, ivies and so on. Soft pastel colours are best for creating an illusion of space, although points of really bright colour, such as those of geraniums (pelargoniums) growing in pots, provide an almost Mediterranean touch.

The single colour of the wisteria is sufficient for the pergola and, again, will maintain the sense of space, which would be lost if several distinctly different climbers were used. A rose, honeysuckle, summer jasmine or other trailing plants make good alternatives.

INDEX AND ACKNOWLEDGEMENTS

Picture credits

Pat Brindley: 9(b),26(t,b),34.
John Glover: 4,41(b).
S & O Mathews: 15,33,35,37(t).
Harry Smith Horticultural Photographic Collection: 1,12,
14,16,19,24,28,29(b),30(t,b),32,40,41(t),43,44,45(t,b),46(t,b).
Michael Warren: 18,20,22,36,37(b),39.

Artwork by Simon Roulstone   **Garden plans by** Robin Williams